ACID RAIN

Sally Morgan

W

FRANKLIN WATTS
A Division of Grolier Publishing
NEW YORK • LONDON • HONG KONG • SYDNEY
DANBURY, CONNECTICUT

Picture Credits

Ecoscene: cover main photo (Sally Morgan), and pages 1 (Sally Morgan), 5 top (Angela Hampton), 9 top (Winkley), 16, 17 bottom (Meissner), 19 bottom (Anthony Cooper), 20 (Andrew Brown), 23 top (Anthony Cooper), 28 (Ian Harwood). **Environmental Images:** pages 11 bottom (Matt Sampson), 24 (Leslie Garland), 25 top (Martin Bond), 25 bottom (Daniel Beltra). **Oxford Scientific Films:** cover small photo (Niall Benvie) and pages 5 bottom (Mike Slater), 6 (Kathie Atkinson), 7 (Carson Baldwin Jr.), 9 bottom (Michael Leach), 14 (David Cayless), 15 top (G. I. Bernard), 19 top (Lena Beyer), 20 top (Barrie E. Watts), 22 (Survival Anglia/John Harris), 23 bottom (Marty Cordano), 26 (Okapia/Kjell-Arne Larsson), 27 top (Okapia). **Panos Pictures:** pages 11 top (J. Holmes). **Planet Earth Pictures:** page 27 bottom (Norbert Wu). **Science Photo Library, London:** pages 4-5 (Simon Fraser), 8-9 (John Mead), 17 top (Martin Bond), 21 bottom (Simon Fraser), 29 top (Astrid & Hanns-Frieder Michler). **Stock Market Photo Library, Inc.:** cover globe image and pages 12, 15 bottom, 18, 29 bottom.

Artwork: Raymond Turvey

EARTH WATCH: ACID RAIN was produced for Franklin Watts by Bender Richardson White.
Project Editor: Lionel Bender
Text Editor: Jenny Vaughan
Designer: Ben White
Picture Researchers: Cathy Stastny and Daniela Marceddu
Media Conversion and Make-Up: MW Graphics, and Clare Oliver
Cover Make-Up: Mike Pilley, Pelican Graphics
Production Controller: Kim Richardson

For Franklin Watts:
Series Editor: Sarah Snashall
Art Director: Robert Walster
Cover Design: Jason Anscomb

First published in 1999 by Franklin Watts

First American edition 1999 by Franklin Watts
A Division of Grolier Publishing
90 Sherman Turnpike
Danbury, CT 06816

Visit Franklin Watts on the Internet at:
http://publishing.grolier.com

Library of Congress Cataloging-in-Publication Data
Morgan, Sally

      Acid Rain/Sally Morgan.--1st American ed.

      p. cm. -- (Earth watch)

  Includes index.

  Summary: Describes the causes of acid rain, its harmful effects, and efforts being made to solve this environmental problem.

  ISBN 0-531-14567-0

  1. Acid rain-- Environmental aspects -- Juvenile literature.

[1. Acid rain. 2. Pollution.] I. Title.

  TD195.44.M67 1999

  363.738'6--dc21

98-52903

CIP

AC

CONTENTS

THE PROBLEM

All around the world, trees and even whole forests are dying. Fish are disappearing from lakes, and buildings are being damaged. This is happening because of a kind of pollution called acid rain.

These trees were killed by acid rain created by waste gases from the power plant.

Polluting the Rain

Acid rain is formed by pollution (damaging substances) in the air. As factories, power plants, and cars burn fuels, they release waste gases. The gases mix with water in the air, so that the rain is also polluted. This polluted water falls to the ground. It harms plants and makes lakes and rivers unsuitable for plants and animals to live in.

What Is Acid Rain?

Acids are liquids that have a sour taste and a strong smell. Some acids exist naturally, others are made in industry. Strong acids are dangerous and can burn a person's skin and even wear away metals. The gases released by burning fuels mix with water in the air and form a weak acid that falls as rain—acid rain.

4

Dipping nets in a pond can help you find out whether acid rain is damaging the plant and animal life in the water.

Nothing New

Acid rain is not a new form of pollution. It has been with us for a long time. It first appeared when people started to burn coal in large quantities approximately 200 years ago. Burning coal releases a number of gases that produce acid rain.

Now people burn oil and natural gas as well as coal, and these also produce acid rain. Luckily, scientists have found ways to stop the damage and to repair the harm that has already been done.

Acid rain has eaten away the surface of this statue in Italy.

5

THE WATER CYCLE

The earth is a watery planet. Two-thirds of its surface is covered by water—mostly salt water in the oceans. Only a small amount is fresh water. The fresh water is mainly ice, but just a little is liquid water in wells, ponds, rivers, and lakes.

Rainwater fills streams and rivers, which eventually empty into lakes or the oceans.

Solid, Liquid, and Gas

Water exists in nature as a solid, called ice; as a liquid, called water; and as a gas, called water vapor. When water is heated, it changes into water vapor, which mixes with the air. We call this process evaporation. When the water vapor cools, it changes back into water. This is called condensation. These processes are happening on the earth's surface all the time.

How Does Rain Form?

The sun's heat evaporates water from the land, rivers, and oceans. It rises into the air as water vapor. As it rises, it cools and condenses to form clouds. Water in the clouds falls back to the ground as rain or snow.

6

Rainwater falling from the sky onto the branch of a tree.

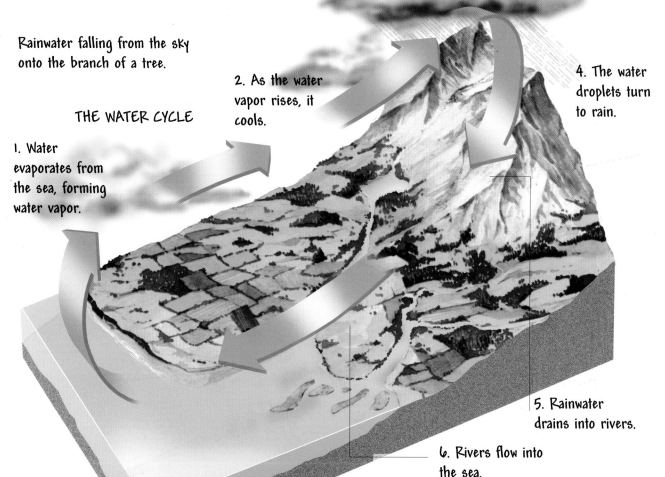

3. It turns to tiny droplets, and forms clouds.

4. The water droplets turn to rain.

THE WATER CYCLE

2. As the water vapor rises, it cools.

1. Water evaporates from the sea, forming water vapor.

5. Rainwater drains into rivers.

6. Rivers flow into the sea.

Taking Part

On a frosty morning, breathe out onto a cold surface such as a windowpane. Your breath will cloud the glass. After a while you will spot tiny drops of water running down the glass. Water vapor in your breath has been cooled by the cold glass and has condensed into water.

Back to the Oceans

Rainwater soaks into the soil and is taken up by plant roots. Some seeps deeper into the ground. The water drains from the land into streams and rivers. Rivers carry the water to the oceans. The cycle starts again when the water evaporates back into the air.

7

ACID OR ALKALINE?

A drop of lemon juice on your tongue tastes sour. So does vinegar. This is because they are both acids. The opposite of an acid is an alkali. Alkalies, such as soap and baking powder, taste bitter and feel soapy.

When polluting gases combine with water droplets in clouds, acid rain is formed.

Strong and Weak Acids

There are many types of acids. There are strong ones used in chemical laboratories, for example sulfuric acid, nitric acid, and hydrochloric acid, and weak ones, such as lemon juice, apple juice, and vinegar.

Acidity (how acidic something is) is measured in units call pH. Chemicals like acids can measure up to 14 on this scale. Acids range from 1 to 6. Strong acids have a pH of 1 or 2. Medium-strength ones such as vinegar may have a pH of about 3. Weak acids, such as apple juice, may have a pH of 5.

Eco Thought
Polluted rainwater can have a pH as low as 2.4, which is as acidic as lemon juice. Mist and snow can be even more acidic.

8

Alkalies

Alkalies are the opposite of acids. Alkaline substances have a pH between 8 and 14. Soap and toothpaste are alkalies. They have a pH of about 9. Bleach has a pH of about 11 or 12.

Neutral Substances

A liquid that has a pH of 7 is neither acidic nor alkaline—it is neutral. If you add an alkali to an acid, it will cancel out the acidity, or neutralize it. For example, some stomachaches are caused by too much acid in the stomach. As a cure, you take a medicine that contains a weak alkali to neutralize the stomach acid.

Hot springs are a natural source of gases that produce acid rain.

Acid rain can make pond water harmful to living things.

ACID RAIN FORMATION

Pure water is neutral and has a pH of 7. However, clean rainwater is slightly acidic. Carbon dioxide—a gas normally present in air—mixes with water vapor to form carbonic acid. This gives rainwater a pH of between 5 and 6. Acid rain may have a pH of 4.

Sources of Pollution

Acid rain is produced mainly by gases known as sulfur dioxide and nitrogen oxides. Some sulfur dioxide comes from natural sources. Volcanoes, hot springs, rotting plant material, sea spray, and even microscopic (very tiny) animals all produce sulfur dioxide. However, most of this gas, and all nitrogen oxides, are produced artificially when various fuels are burned.

ACID RAIN AROUND THE WORLD
- Source of air pollution
- Some acid rain problems
- Serious acid rain problems

From Gas to Acid

Fossil fuels, which include coal, oil, and natural gas, are the major sources of polluting gases the world over. Coal contains the chemical sulfur. When this burns, it combines with oxygen in the air to form sulfur dioxide. This gas, mixed with water vapor, produces sulfuric acid. In a similar way, nitrogen from fuels combines with oxygen to make nitrogen oxides and nitric acid. Hydrocarbons produce carbon dioxide gas and carbonic acid.

Eco Thought
One-seventh of the material making up coal is the chemical sulfur. Sulfur makes up less than a hundredth of oil and gas, so these produce far less air pollution than coal.

10

People in Thailand try to protect themselves from car exhaust gases. These include nitrogen oxide, which can cause acid rain.

On the Ground

Polluting gases mix in the air to form ozone. This gas can cause breathing difficulties in people and damage to plants. Ground-level ozone is harmful, but ozone high in the sky is good.

Into the Atmosphere

Fossil fuels are burned in power plants to produce electricity. The electricity is used to heat and light homes, schools, and offices, and to drive machines in factories. Vehicles burn gasoline or diesel oil as fuels. The waste gases rise into the air.

The Action of Sunlight

Some of the sulfur dioxide and nitrogen oxides released by power plants falls back to the ground. But most rises high into the atmosphere. There, the sun's strong rays help the gases mix with water vapor to form acid rain.

A mix of polluting gases forms a smog, or thick, dirty cloud, over some cities.

CARRIED ON WINDS

Nearer the ground, the wind is slowed down by trees, houses, and other obstacles. High in the sky, where there is nothing to slow it down, it blows much faster.

Chimney Height

Until about 150 years ago, factories had short chimneys. Air pollution was released near the ground and settled over the surrounding land. This made plants and animals unhealthy.

To overcome the problem, people built very tall chimneys to send pollution high into the sky. But this means that the pollution stays in the air longer, and creates more acid rain. Strong winds carry the polluted air over long distances.

The air pollution from this factory in Scotland rises from chimneys.

12

THE ACID RAIN CYCLE

Winds carry the gases many miles away, where they eventually form clouds.

Fumes from power plants, factories, and vehicles rise into the air.

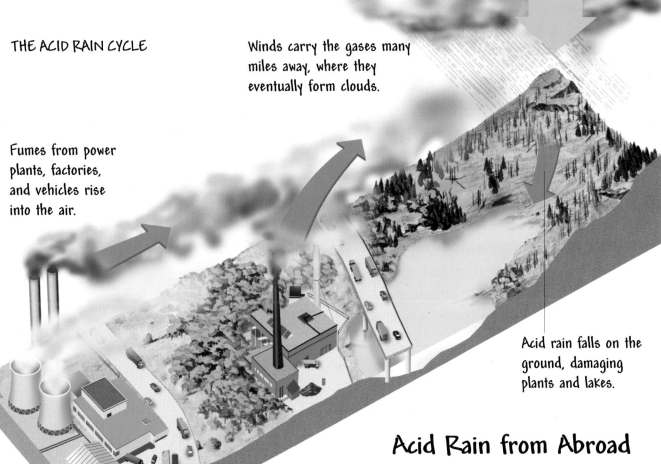

Acid rain falls on the ground, damaging plants and lakes.

Acid Rain from Abroad

Acid rain does not only affect the countries that produce it. In Europe, for example, polluted air from Britain is carried by the wind to Norway and Sweden. Nine-tenths of acid rain that falls on Norway comes from abroad. In North America, remote regions of Canada get acid rain produced by industry in the United States.

Acid rain is a world problem, and nations have to work together to solve it.

Taking Part

Pollution from a chimney 33 feet (10 meters) high travels about 75 miles (120 kilometers) in a day. Pollution from a chimney 164 feet (50 meters) high travels about 105 miles (170 kilometers). Use a map to see where winds will carry the pollution.

ACID SOIL AND WATER

When acid rain falls to the ground, the water may soak into the soil or it may drain into streams, rivers, and lakes. This way it affects the acidity of both the soil and the water.

Only one-fiftieth of the world's water is fresh, like this lake water, so it is essential to keep it acid-free.

Falling on Soil

Not all soils are the same. Chalky soils are alkaline. When acid rain falls on these, the acids are neutralized (made into a neutral substance) and do not do much damage.

Soils in mountain areas are often quite acidic. Where there are conifer trees, such as pines, their needle-like leaves fall to the ground and these make soil acidic, too. When acid rain falls on acid soils, the soils become even more acidic.

On the Ground

In the Adirondack Mountains of the northeastern United States, the soils are naturally acidic. This and acid rain has made the lakes extremely acidic. One of the lakes there has a pH of 4.2.

14

Washing Out the Nutrients

Soils contain nutrients (chemicals that help plants stay healthy). Plants use their roots to draw up these substances from the soil.

Acid rain can wash nutrients away, and the plants can starve. It also makes it possible for toxic (poisonous) substances in the soil to get into the soil water. The water drains into rivers and lakes, making them poisonous. The poisons can also get into plants as they take up the water in their roots.

These seedlings have sent up green shoots to make food and have grown long roots to take up nutrients from the soil.

Scientists in Britain test lake water to see if it has been polluted by acid rain. They use meters that measure the pH of the water.

15

DYING TREES

Acid rain affects all plants, but trees are suffering the most. Around the world, millions of trees are under attack from acid rain. The trees at the greatest risk are conifer trees.

A row of plane trees by a lake in Hungary. Acid rain has caused all the leaves to fall off.

The First Signs

Acid rain weakens trees. It does this partly by washing nutrients from the soil so that the trees grow much slower than normal. It also releases harmful chemicals from the soil, which are taken up by the trees' roots. This makes the leaves fall off. Plants need leaves to make food from sunlight.

Eco Thought

In Germany, it is estimated that it may cost as much as $25 billion to reduce the effects of acid rain on forest soils and lakes so that trees may once again grow normally and healthily.

16

A scientist studies trees protected from acid rain to compare their growth with trees in the open.

Dieback

With fewer leaves, plants make less food. Pests and droughts are more likely to damage them, and branches start to die. This is called dieback. Eventually, the whole tree might die.

Foresters used to clear hillsides of dying trees and their roots, replacing them with new trees. Now, they leave roots and branches, as they have found that these release alkalies when they rot and help reduce acidity in the soil.

Taking Part

Line two plastic containers with paper towels. Sprinkle some water and cress seeds over the paper. After a few days the seeds should germinate (sprout). Then water one container with rainwater, and the other with lemon juice. Watch what happens over the next few days.

At the tips of the branches of this conifer tree, the leaves have turned brown because of damage from acid rain.

17

DYING LAKES

If acid rain falls onto the surface of a lake or drains into the lake from the surrounding land, the water in the lake becomes more acidic.

Eggs and Acid Rain

The animals of a lake are the first to be affected by the acid rain. As the water in the lake becomes more acidic, the eggs of fish and amphibians (animals such as frogs, newts, and toads) become damaged and may not hatch.

On the Ground

Very blue water in a lake is usually a sign of acid rain damage. A healthy lake has murky water due to the mass of microscopic life living in it.

Acid rain has killed most of the plants and animals in this lake in Germany. It has also damaged the trees around it.

This water lily is one of the few plants surviving in a lake in Sweden with an acid level of pH 4.8.

The number of frogs in the world is falling. Scientists think this is due to acid rain damaging frogspawn and killing insects that the adult frogs feed on.

Eco Thought

More than 15,000 lakes in Sweden have been damaged by acid rain, and 4,000 of these lakes no longer have any fish in them.

Poison in the Water

Freshwater shrimps and some other animals have a tough outer covering on their bodies called an exoskeleton. A substance called calcium makes this hard. Acid wears away the calcium in the exoskeleton and the animal inside it dies.

Aluminum normally present in soil may be washed into the lake from the surrounding land by acid rain. Aluminum poisons fish, especially trout and salmon. It damages their gills so they cannot breathe in the water.

Food Chains

The different kinds of living things in a lake depend on each other. When one is killed by the acidity, the others are affected. For example, fish eat shrimps and herons eat fish. If the shrimps die, the fish will starve, and so will the herons. Slowly, the animal life in the lake disappears.

DAMAGED STONE

Many buildings are made of stone. Some kinds of stone are quite soft and can be damaged by naturally acidic rainwater. Acid rain makes the problem worse.

Attacking Stone

Two kinds of stone that are easily damaged are limestone and sandstone. They are lightweight, attractive in color, and easy to cut and shape. However, over hundreds of years, rain erodes, or wears away, the surface of the stone. Acid rain speeds up this erosion. Carvings lose their features, and the arms and feet of statues weaken and drop off. The stone turns black and looks dirty.

This sandstone canyon in the United States has been worn away naturally by the effects of rainwater.

Limiting the Damage

Because acid rain removes the surface of stone, not much can be done to repair the damage. Worn stone can be replaced, and walls can be cleaned. However, a special substance can be painted over stone to protect it from erosion by rain.

The acids also wear away the surface of plastics, stained-glass windows, electrical equipment, and metal on buildings. Even paintings inside art galleries are affected. Galleries and museums have special air-conditioning units to remove the acidic gases.

Lichens grow on rocks, walls, and trees. They are one of the first living things to be killed by acid rain.

Taking Part

Find two pieces of chalk. Drip a few drops of water onto one piece and vinegar onto the other and watch the different reactions. The acid in the vinegar attacks the chalk, fizzing as it makes contact. The gas, carbon dioxide, is given off. The water does nothing.

A craftsman repairs damage caused by acid rain to stonework on a church in Poland.

Eco Thought

In the last 25 years, air pollution has done more damage to the ancient statues and buildings in the city of Athens, Greece, than in the 2,500 years before that.

HARMFUL POLLUTANTS

Acid rain looks, feels, and tastes just like clean rain. And it is safe to walk in acid rain. It is the air pollutants creating acid rain that can seriously damage people's health.

Air pollution can create a cloud of dirt and fumes, like this one over Mexico City.

Breathing in Polluted Air

If we breathe in the gases sulfur dioxide and nitrogen oxides, our lungs can be damaged. This is most serious for people who have breathing problems, such as asthma. When the levels of air pollution are high, these people are often warned not to go outside.

An asthma sufferer uses an inhaler to help her breathe.

Eco Thought

During the winter of 1952, there was a thick smog over London, England, caused by sulfur dioxide and soot from coal fires people used to heat their homes. Thousands of people died from breathing problems.

City Air and Trees

The problem of air pollution builds up in city centers, where the exhaust from traffic mixes with chemicals from factories and power plants. All these polluting gases together seriously affect our health. The effects are worst on sunny days when there is no wind. A dirty yellow haze called smog forms above cities. This can hang over a city for days on end.

City trees can help remove some of the air pollution. Their leaves take up some of the polluting gases. Some city trees are better at surviving air pollution than others. For example, the bark of the London plane tree collects poisonous substances from within the tree. The bark then peels off, saving the tree from dying.

This man takes readings from a machine that measures pollution levels in the air, so people with breathing problems can be warned when these are high.

23

SOLVING THE PROBLEM

To reduce acid rain, we must produce less polluting gases in the air. The amount of sulfur dioxide released into the air has been falling since 1970. But the amount of nitrogen oxides has been increasing as the number of vehicles on the roads increases.

Reducing Pollution

Many countries now have laws that limit the amount of air pollution that power plants, industry, and cars can produce. Power plants burning fossil fuels can reduce the amount of sulfur dioxide they produce by burning oil or coal with less sulfur in it. They can also fit filters on chimneys to remove polluting gases.

Taking Part

Try to find out about the fuel your local power plant uses. Does it use coal, gas, or nuclear energy, or does it produce electricity using non-polluting energy sources?

A filter in this new power plant chimney will remove sulfur dioxide from the gases given off when coal is burned.

Renewable Energy

New power plants can be built that use the energy of wind, water, or the sun (solar power). These do not produce any air pollution, and the sources of energy can be used over and over again.

Cleaner Cars

Modern cars burn fuel more efficiently than older ones. New cars are fitted with a catalytic converter as part of the exhaust system. Waste gases from the engine are made harmless as they pass through the converter.

In this Canadian hydroelectric power plant, water gushing through pipes in the dam turns turbines (motors) to generate electricity.

Here, wind energy turns turbines that make electricity. Wind power is a renewable source of energy.

25

OVERCOMING THE ACID

In many countries, people are battling to repair the damage caused by acid rain. They do this by trying to get rid of the acid from the soil and water.

Alkaline lime is spread on this moorland in Sweden to help neutralize the acid.

Treating the Soil

The soil on many farms is naturally slightly acidic. Farmers spread lime on the soil to make it less acidic and to help plants grow. Lime is an alkaline substance. It balances the acid in the soil to make the pH of the soil neutral.

Soil and water damaged by acid rain can be treated in a similar way. Lime is spread over the soil, and rain washes it into the ground. Helicopters drop lime over lakes. This has to be done every two years, because rain keeps adding acid to the water.

Taking Part

Many water companies have found that the water they take from rivers and lakes is quite acidic and must be treated. Try finding out if your local water company has to get rid of acidity in the water.

26

A sample of water from a lake is tested for purity and acidity.

On the Ground

In 1990, the U.S. government started the Acid Rain Program. It aimed to reduce over many years the amount of sulfur dioxide and nitrogen oxides being produced. It is succeeding in helping to save the forests and lakes from further acid rain damage.

Replacing Lost Fish

In the 1980s, brown trout started to disappear from Norway's lakes and rivers. The fish were being killed by the acidic water. Now, scientists have found that some types of brown trout are better able to live in the acidic waters. These types are being bred to produce more fish. One day some of the lifeless acid lakes will be restocked with these brown trout.

A brown trout that can live in acidic waters.

27

HEALTH CHECK

Does your part of the world get acid rain? Scientists use special instruments to check the quality of air, soil, and water. But the effects of acid rain can easily be seen by looking at the trees and buildings in an area.

These trees are being checked for signs of acid rain damage, such as dead leaves or branches.

Looking for Damage

Conifer, silver birch, and beech trees are the worst affected. The best time to check the health of any tree is in early summer, when it carries the most leaves.

The first signs of damage are yellow, blotchy leaves and some branches without any leaves. A badly damaged tree has many dead branches and leathery, rolled-up leaves. The tree becomes so weakened that it is easily attacked by insect pests and diseases.

Taking Part

Acid rain eats away the stone of buildings, leaving large cracks and holes. The faces of statues lose their eyes and noses. In your area, see if there are any differences in the condition of older stones compared with newer ones.

28

What Can You Do?

Cycling and walking to work or school, instead of using cars, helps keep you fit and healthy, but it also helps save energy and makes less air pollution.

In the home, energy can be saved by switching off lights and machines when they are not in use. Recycling or reusing bottles, jars, and paper cuts down the amount of energy needed to make these items. Anything that means that less coal, oil, or gas is burned will greatly help reduce the problems of acid rain.

This catalytic converter removes many polluting gases from car exhausts.

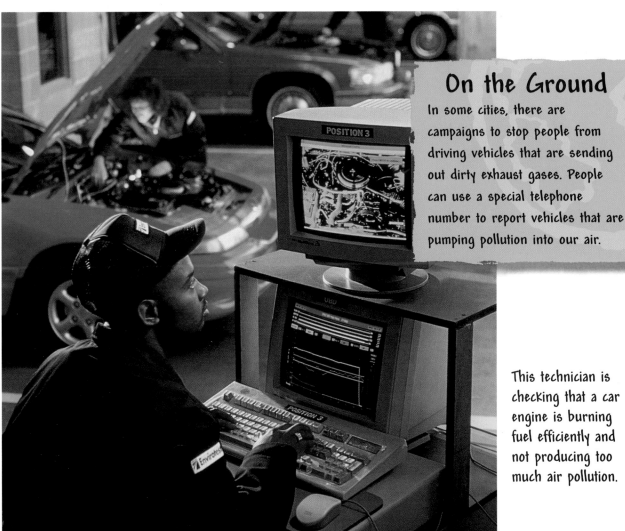

On the Ground

In some cities, there are campaigns to stop people from driving vehicles that are sending out dirty exhaust gases. People can use a special telephone number to report vehicles that are pumping pollution into our air.

This technician is checking that a car engine is burning fuel efficiently and not producing too much air pollution.

29

FACT FILE

Rock Erosion

Caves are often formed where rain soaks through cracks in rocks and erodes (wears away) the rock around them. This happens naturally where the rain is slightly acidic because it is mixed in with the gas carbon dioxide. Over thousands of years, this water carves out a cave. The largest single cave in the world is on the island of Borneo. Its inside is so large that there is enough space to park 8,000 trucks.

Much More Acid

On average, the rain in Europe now contains more than 70 times more acid than it did in 1950.

Damaged Forests

In Great Britain and Germany, more than half the forests have been damaged by acid rain.

Troubled Areas

The worst acid rain problems are in northern and central Europe, North America, central Russia, Mexico, Australia, Japan, and China.

Lack of Fish

Acid rain is killing trout in New York State, U.S.A. This is damaging the tourist industry because people are not coming to the state to fish.

Swedish Efforts

Between 1970 and 1988, Sweden managed to reduce the amount of sulfur dioxide it created by three-quarters.

Science in Action

Scientists believe that the latest designs of filters fitted to cars exhausts and to the chimneys of power plants and incinerators will help to cut sulfur dioxide production in Europe by four-fifths.

Number of Cars

Between 1950 and 1990, the number of road vehicles in the world increased by ten times, and the number is still increasing. Today, there are believed to be at least 550 million vehicles on the world's roads.

Polluted Drinking Water

Acid rain can lead to polluted drinking water. Any acid in our drinking water attacks the metal in old water pipes. Poisonous metals such as aluminum, lead, and copper may be released into the water. These metals can make people ill, discolor their hair or damage it so that it falls out, and cause serious brain damage.

GLOSSARY

Acid A substance that has a pH of less than 7. Acids can be strong and dangerous to touch, or weak, like lemon juice, vinegar, or acid rain.

Alkali A substance with a pH greater than 7, for example, bleach, ammonia, or soap.

Alkaline Containing an alkali or alkalies.

Asthma A problem some people have that sometimes makes it very difficult to breathe normally.

Atmosphere The layer of gases around the earth.

Carbon dioxide A gas in the air made up of a substance called carbon and the gas oxygen. We give out carbon dioxide when we breathe. The gas is released when coal, oil, or natural gas is burned.

Condensation Liquid formed by a gas such as water vapor when it cools.

Condense A change in state from a gas to a liquid, such as water vapor changing back to liquid water.

Evaporation A change in state from liquid to a gas, for example, when liquid water

turns into water vapor in the atmosphere.

Exhaust The waste gases pumped out by the engines of all kinds of vehicles.

Fossil fuels Fuels such as coal and oil that have been made from the bodies of plants and animals that died millions of years ago.

Generator A machine for making electricity. It changes the energy of a turning wheel into electrical energy.

Germinate When a plant begins to sprout and grow.

Hydrocarbon A substance that contains only carbon and hydrogen gas. There are hydrocarbons in coal and natural gas.

Hydroelectric Electricity made by harnessing the energy of moving water.

Lime A white alkaline powder, often used by farmers to make soil less acidic.

Limestone A kind of rock. If limestone is heated, the substance lime is produced.

Neutral Neither acidic nor alkaline, having a pH of 7.

Neutralize To reduce the acidity or alkalinity so that it becomes neither acidic nor alkaline.

Nitrogen oxide One of the gases that forms acid rain.

Nutrients Substances living things need to help them grow and stay healthy.

Ozone A gas. A layer of ozone high in the atmosphere protects the earth from harmful rays from the sun.

pH The unit for measuring acidity, ranging from 1 to 14.

Pollution Dirt and damaging substances in the environment.

Smog A yellow haze lying over cities, created by pollution from industry and cars.

Sulfur dioxide A gas that forms acid rain.

Toxic Poisonous.

Turbine A motor with a set of blades that are turned by moving gas or liquid.

Water vapor Water in the form of a gas. There is water vapor in clouds and in the air we breathe.

INDEX

J
363.
738
MOR

Morgan, Sally.

Acid rain.

9/00

$20.25 Grades 2-3

DATE		
DISCARD		

LINDENHURST MEMORIAL LIBRARY
LINDENHURST, NEW YORK 11757

BAKER & TAYLOR